Benjamin Banneker

History Maker Bios

Catherine A. Welch

⌐ LERNER PUBLICATIONS COMPANY • MINNEAPOLIS

To my mother and father, hardworking and honest people

The author wishes to thank Judith Stark, Raymond Bouley, Jackie Hoffman, and the staff of the Southbury, Connecticut, library for their assistance in gathering material for this book.

Text copyright © 2008 by Catherine A. Welch
Illustrations copyright © 2008 by Publishing Group, Inc.

Illustrations by Tad Butler

Lerner Publications Company
A division of Lerner Publishing Group, Inc.
241 First Avenue North
Minneapolis, MN 55401 USA

Website address: www.lernerbooks.com

Library of Congress Cataloging-in-Publication Data

Welch, Catherine A.
    Benjamin Banneker / by Catherine A. Welch.
      p.   cm. — (History maker biographies)
    Includes bibliographical references and index.
    ISBN 978–0–8225–7167–4 (lib. bdg. : alk. paper)
    1. Banneker, Benjamin, 1731–1806—Juvenile literature. 2. Astronomers—United States—Biography—Juvenile literature. 3. African American scientists—Biography—Juvenile literature. I. Title.
QB36.B22W46 2008
520.92—dc22 [B]   2007025216

Manufactured in the United States of America
1 2 3 4 5 6 – JR – 13 12 11 10 09 08

TABLE OF CONTENTS

INTRODUCTION

Benjamin Banneker was an African American mathematician and astronomer. He was born in the British colony of Maryland on November 9, 1731. At that time, most blacks in the colonies were slaves. Banneker's father and grandfather were once slaves.

In the 1700s, many people did not think African Americans had great minds for science or mathematics. Banneker showed that these people were wrong. In fact, he was one of the smartest people of his day.

This is his story.

1 FAMILY AND CHORES

Benjamin Banneker had the dark skin of a black slave. Like slave children, he did chores on a tobacco farm. But he was never a slave. His father, Robert, owned their tobacco farm in Baltimore County, Maryland.

At that time, few free blacks owned land. But when Benjamin was six, his father bought a one-hundred-acre farm called Stout. Robert traded seven thousand pounds of tobacco for the land. He put Benjamin's name on the deed. He wanted Benjamin to get the land when he died.

Some free blacks owned slaves. But Robert and his wife, Mary, had no slave workers. Benjamin and his four sisters helped with the tobacco crops. Benjamin chopped out weeds with a hoe. He picked worms and caterpillars off tobacco leaves.

Robert Banneker put Benjamin's name on this deed for his farm. It is dated March 8, 1737.

Young Benjamin worked hard with his hands. But he found ways to use his mind, too. He loved numbers. He thought about the number of jobs done to raise a tobacco crop. There were at least thirty-six different chores.

Benjamin did many farm chores. He cleaned and fed farm animals. He planted corn, cleared roots and rocks from the land, and repaired fences. Sometimes he went hunting and fishing with his father.

FAMILY ROOTS

Molly Welsh, a white Englishwoman, owned a farm in Maryland and two slaves. She eventually freed the slaves. One slave, called Bannka, was later known as Banneky. His daughter, Mary, married Robert, a freed slave. He took Mary's last name, Banneky. Later, the family began using the spelling, "Banneker."

This illustration is from the late 1700s. It shows how tobacco leaves were dried and sorted at a tobacco farm.

Some people saw that Benjamin could do more than farm chores. His grandmother may have taught him to read and write. He learned quickly and had a great memory. He learned to read, write, and speak like the educated white colonists. Eventually, Benjamin went to school.

The teacher at the one-room schoolhouse also helped Benjamin. The teacher was a Quaker. Many Quakers wanted to stop slavery, and they often helped blacks. At school, Benjamin met several white children. He also met Jacob Hall, another free black.

RUN AWAY

THE 18th Inftant at Night from the Subfcriber, in the City of New-York, four Negro Men, Viz. LESTER, about 40 Years of Age, had on a white Flannel Jacket and Drawers, Duck Trowfers and Home-fpun Shirt. CÆSAR, about 18 Years of Age, cloathed in the fame Manner. ISAAC, aged 17 Years cloathed in the fame Manner, except that his Breeches were Leather; and MINGO, 15 Years of Age, with the the fame Clothing as the 2 firft, all of them of a middling Size, Whoever delivers either of the faid Negroes to the Subfcriber, fhall receive TWENTY SHILLINGS Reward for each befide all reafonable Charges. If any perfon can give Intelligence of their being harbour'd, a reward of TEN POUNDS will be paid upon conviction of the Offender. All Mafters of Veffels and others are forewarn'd not to Tranfport them from the City, as I am refolved to profecute

This newspaper ad describes four runaway slaves. It offers a reward to anyone who returns them to the owner.

Jacob and Benjamin became good friends. But Benjamin met few other people. The white neighbors did not welcome free African Americans to social gatherings. The Banneker family kept to themselves. They lived in fear of some whites.

Free blacks feared slave catchers. These people looked for runaway slaves. But some whites also snatched free blacks and sold them as slaves. They even grabbed black children. Perhaps slave catchers may have tried to take Benjamin as a child.

Young Benjamin's family did not share his love of numbers and reading. As a boy, he had no books of his own. He borrowed books. And he learned by looking at the world and thinking. He was curious, and he was a genius. He could discover things for himself.

When he was about twenty, he thought about time. In colonial days, clocks and watches were rare. People used sundials. But few people kept track of the time each hour. Benjamin borrowed a pocket watch from a merchant or traveler. He studied its many parts carefully.

Colonial people used sundials like this one to tell time. The shadows move along the dial's face as the sun moves through the sky.

He studied how each wheel and gear worked. He memorized every detail of the watch. Then he went home and made a drawing of the clock's workings.

In his spare time, he used a pocket knife to make a clock. He carved the clock parts from wood. He did not know if a large clock could be made of wood. He had never seen one before. But in 1753, he completed a clock that worked! His clock had a bell that struck on the hour.

This wooden clock is similar to the one that Benjamin made.

Benjamin's neighbors were amazed that he could do this. Only a few colonists understood how to build a clock. Most would not even spend the time trying. But Benjamin loved the challenge. It was like doing a puzzle. He loved puzzles.

However, Benjamin did not have much time for puzzles after 1759. His father died that year. At twenty-eight, Benjamin had to take charge of the farm. He had to care for his mother and sisters.

2 NEIGHBORS, WORK, AND STUDY

After his sisters married, Benjamin lived alone with his mother. He had little in common with slave workers. Few slaves could read and write. In some colonies, laws stopped slaves from learning how to read and write. But like many slaves, Benjamin enjoyed music. He owned a flute and a violin.

At times, white neighbors came to see his clock. Some asked him to help them read and write letters. Benjamin was happy to help. But he led a life apart from his white neighbors.

Then the Ellicotts, a white Quaker family, moved into the area. They bought and cleared land. They had big plans for their land. They built mills along the Patapsco River.

Fear of Slave Uprisings

During Benjamin's lifetime, life for African Americans got worse. Whites feared that slaves would revolt or escape in great numbers. Laws were passed in Maryland to control all blacks. Free African Americans had to carry papers to prove they were free. A black person needed a permit to own a gun or even a dog.

The Ellicotts' workers improved the rough roads. They built dams and a bridge. Benjamin heard the muffled sounds of the Ellicotts' workers a mile away. By this time, he was forty years old. The activity gave him new things to think about.

Why were the Ellicotts building gristmills? The gristmills were used to turn grain into flour. But the local people did not grow grain.

Everyone watched the Ellicotts plant fields of wheat and sell flour. Soon, Benjamin's neighbors saw they could make money growing wheat. They began planting wheat and selling it to the Ellicotts.

The Ellicotts built their mills along the Patapsco River (BELOW). They used waterpower to grind the grain.

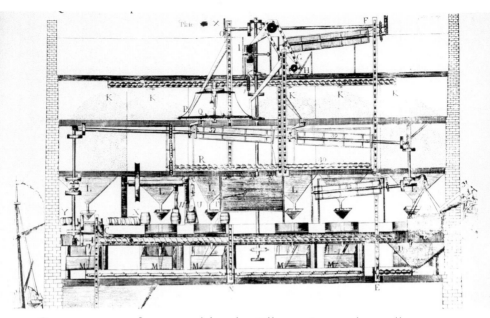

Benjamin was fascinated by the Ellicotts' complex milling machines. This diagram shows the inside of one of their mills.

Benjamin wasn't as quick to start growing wheat. But he found the mills exciting. Benjamin saw machines take bags of grain from the wagons. He watched machines raise the bags to the highest part of the mill. He studied how grain was emptied onto the millstones. What would the machines do next? Benjamin kept watching.

Benjamin wanted to meet the Ellicotts. He knew he could learn a lot from them. But the Ellicotts were white. He took his time getting to know them.

The Ellicott store (LEFT) sat next to the homes of John Ellicott (CENTER) and Jonathan Ellicott (RIGHT).

Meanwhile, the Ellicotts learned about Benjamin. They were eager to meet him. His farm was near their workers' boardinghouse. The workers needed food. Benjamin and his mother gladly sold them poultry, vegetables, fruit, and honey.

The Ellicotts soon built a store with a post office. The store was a great place to meet new people who came into town. It was a place where Benjamin could get a newspaper. There he learned about events in the colonies.

The store was a place for lively conversation. But Benjamin did not speak until others asked him to join the talks. Then he jumped in with lots to say.

By 1776, the American Revolution (1775–1783) was under way. The colonists wanted their freedom from British control. Benjamin and the other African Americans liked this talk of freedom. Maybe it meant slaves would be freed. Benjamin did not fight in the war. But he decided to finally grow some wheat to help the troops.

Benjamin did not fight in the American Revolution, but many African Americans did. Peter Salem (RIGHT), a freed slave, fought at the Battle of Bunker Hill.

During this time, Banneker met George Ellicott. Banneker was forty-seven. George was only eighteen. But they had much in common.

George was as bright and curious as Benjamin. George shared his love for astronomy with Benjamin and the neighbors. Astronomy is the study of stars and other objects in space.

Banneker eagerly listened. George let Benjamin use his telescope. Benjamin also learned about the stars from his friend. A whole new world suddenly opened up for Banneker.

3 STARGAZING

During the next few years, Benjamin couldn't stop looking at the stars and moon. George was thrilled to see his friend becoming an astronomer. In 1788, George let Benjamin borrow some of his books and instruments.

George loaned him a telescope, a pair of compasses, a table, and a tin candleholder. Benjamin felt honored that George trusted him with his expensive tools.

Benjamin read George's books. He figured out how to use the instruments, even though he had no science training. The books were hard to read even for someone *with* science training!

Astronomers recorded their observations of the stars on maps. This map from the 1700s shows the pictures that astronomers used to help remember different star patterns.

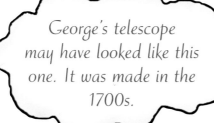

George's telescope may have looked like this one. It was made in the 1700s.

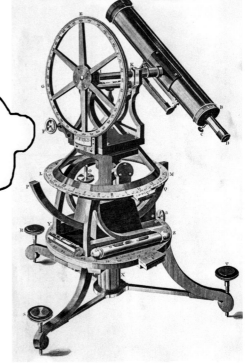

Benjamin figured out how to predict an eclipse of the sun. A solar eclipse happens when the moon passes between Earth and the sun. For a short time, the moon blocks the sun.

At night, Benjamin stayed up with the telescope. In the mornings, he slept late. Some neighbors thought he was getting lazy. Soon his farm suffered. Benjamin got angry with himself. His father had told him that owning land was important. Land gives a person freedom, his father had said. Benjamin kept studying, but he made sure he took care of the farm.

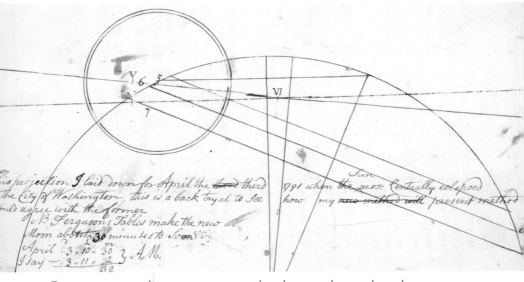

Benjamin used a compass and ruler to draw this diagram
of when an eclipse would take place.

In 1789, Benjamin sent George his work
on the solar eclipse. George was amazed at
what Benjamin had learned by himself.
George found only one mistake. Benjamin
was disappointed that he had made any
mistakes at all. But soon, he was excited
about a new project.

He decided to create an ephemeris. This
is a chart that lists the position of heavenly
bodies each day of the year. The chart
gives facts about the rising and setting of
the sun, the moon, and certain stars.

Colonists needed this information to help them plan. Farmers used it to predict the weather and to choose good dates for planting. In those days, farmers bought almanacs that included this information. Most almanacs had an ephemeris for the year.

Benjamin created an ephemeris for each of the twelve months of 1791. The Ellicotts wanted to see his work published. Benjamin sent the ephemeris to several printers. But he was disappointed when he could not get it published that year.

COLONIAL ALMANACS

Almanacs were published each year. They were sold in bookshops and by traveling sellers. Facts and charts about stars, tides, and weather helped sea captains, fishing crews, and farmers. Colonial families read almanacs for health advice, calendars, poetry, and election dates.

However, soon he had a new challenge ahead of him. The colonists had won the American Revolution. The new nation was planning a place for its capital. The states of Maryland and Virginia agreed to give part of their land for the new capital city.

The city would be ten miles square. In February 1791, President George Washington chose Major Andrew Ellicott to survey (mark) the four ten-mile sides of this land. Andrew wanted his cousin George Ellicott to help him. Andrew needed someone with knowledge of astronomy and scientific instruments to do the surveying.

Andrew Ellicott (LEFT) earned the title Major while fighting in the American Revolution.

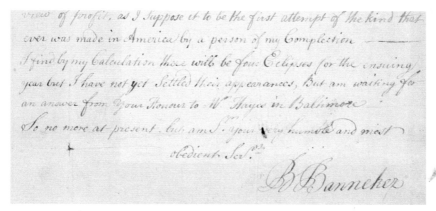

Benjamin knew Andrew Ellicott before they worked together. In 1790, Benjamin wrote this letter to Andrew, asking him to help publish the 1791 ephemeris.

George was too busy at the time. So he suggested Benjamin for the job. Banneker was almost sixty but excited. Most whites would never get such an honor.

Benjamin's sisters agreed to care for his animals and house while he was away. George's wife helped make new clothes for Benjamin. That month, he and Major Ellicott traveled by horseback to Alexandria, Virginia.

Benjamin suffered from stiff, aching joints. The ride was long and painful for him. But the trip was worth it. Alexandria was an exciting town. It was a busy place, full of merchants and sailors.

The Potomac River (ABOVE) carried travelers and merchants from Alexandria to the Atlantic Ocean.

On the wharves, Benjamin watched cargo being loaded and unloaded. And people saw Benjamin, a well-dressed African American with graying, curly hair. They saw him with Major Ellicott. They must have been shocked. How could a black man be part of such an important project?

The land for the new capital was beautiful. Benjamin saw farm fields, pastures, and woods. The Potomac and Anacosta rivers ran by the land. But Benjamin saw that marking the boundaries would be difficult. Would he be able to do his job?

The survey team used a zenith sector to observe the stars. This tool helped them know their spot on the ground. Some stars appeared right overhead. Others seemed at angles to the men. Since Earth constantly moves, angles keep changing.

The team kept track of their spot on the ground. They recorded the time each measurement was taken each day. Banneker had the important job of tending the clock.

The clock caused many problems. If the ground shook nearby, the clock did not record time correctly. The clock also did not work right if the temperature changed.

This is the zenith sector that Benjamin and his team used to take measurements.

Benjamin used this compass to check the position of the sun and stars. It belonged to Andrew Ellicott.

Benjamin used several thermometers to check the temperature of the clock area. He kept the clock wound. He used instruments to check the clock's time with the position of the sun.

Benjamin did much of his work at night. Each hour, he checked the clock against readings of the sky. In his free time at night, he studied the sky for a new ephemeris.

All the men liked Benjamin. They wanted him to eat at their table. But he did not feel he should eat with the white men. He ate in the same tent as the other men. But he ate at a separate small table.

President Washington came to the site to check on the work. Banneker must have seen him. He may have even spoken to the president.

Most of the men slept at night while Benjamin worked. He spent the nights alone in the instrument tent. He got only a few hours of sleep each day.

Benjamin worked seven days a week for over two months. The cold and humid air deepened the pain in his stiff joints. He was happy when the work was done.

Pierre Charles L'Enfant created this 1791 plan of Washington, D.C. Benjamin used it to help lay out the city.

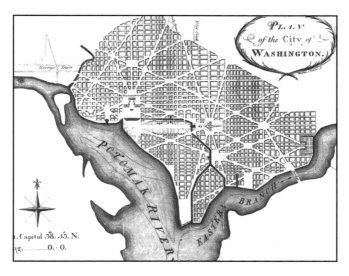

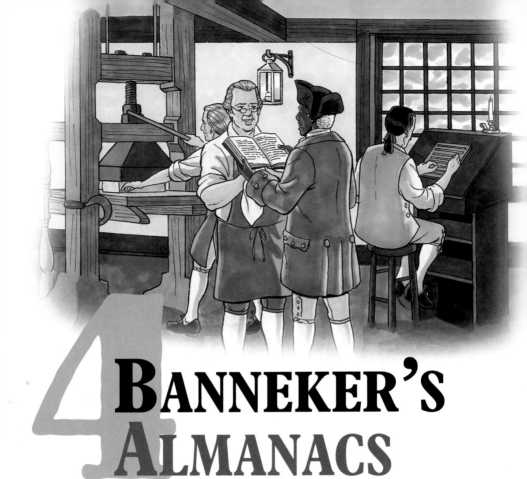

4 BANNEKER'S ALMANACS

When Benjamin returned home, he finished an ephemeris for a 1792 Almanac. He mailed a copy of his work to a printer in Georgetown, Washington, D.C. He also took his work to printers in Baltimore, Maryland, and Philadelphia, Pennsylvania.

George Ellicott and his brother Elias wanted to see Benjamin's almanac printed. They believed it would show that blacks are as smart as whites. It was important to show the talents of an African American. The Ellicotts hoped that Banneker's almanac might even help stop slavery.

Benjamin welcomed help from the Ellicotts. He spoke with others who were also against slavery. They were sure that people would rush to buy his almanac. People would want to see what an African American could write.

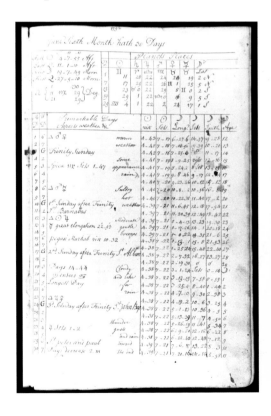

This page from Benjamin's journal shows some of his calculations for his 1792 Almanac.

Benjamin did not want the book to sell just because he was black. But soon, he saw how his almanac might help other blacks. On August 19, 1791, he sent Thomas Jefferson a copy of the almanac and a letter. Jefferson was the secretary of state at the time.

In the letter, Benjamin wrote that he was proud to be of the African race. He was dark, "of the deepest dye." He scolded Jefferson for owning slaves. He challenged Jefferson to think differently about blacks.

JEFFERSON'S THOUGHTS ON SLAVERY

Thomas Jefferson owned slaves and treated them kindly. He thought African Americans were brave and faithful servants. But he did not think blacks had deep feelings and great minds. Jefferson thought slavery was evil and harmed both slaves and masters. He did not think whites and blacks could live together. He suggested that African Americans should be sent away to another country.

Fifteen years earlier, Jefferson had written in the Declaration of Independence that "all men are created equal" But he did not think blacks were equal to whites. Benjamin offered his almanac as proof that blacks and whites are equal.

It took courage for Banneker to write to a powerful man like Jefferson. He did not expect Jefferson to reply to his letter. But Jefferson did.

On August 30, Jefferson wrote a letter to Benjamin. Jefferson welcomed proof that blacks are equal to other people. He wrote that he wanted to improve life for blacks.

Jefferson wrote this letter to Benjamin on August 30, 1791.

He told Benjamin he was sending the almanac to the Academy of Sciences in Paris, France. This was a great honor. People would now learn about Benjamin and his almanac.

The almanac was first printed in Baltimore. It sold many copies. The almanac included a letter from Senator James McHenry of Maryland. McHenry wrote that Banneker was a free black and had done the ephemeris for the almanac. This, he said, was proof that African Americans had great minds and talents.

James McHenry was born in Ireland. He came to the United States to work as an army doctor. He stayed in Maryland and served for many years as a politician.

The *1792 Almanack* included the times for the rising and setting of the sun and moon. It had dates for eclipses of the sun. Weather forecasts and dates for yearly feasts were also included. Readers also saw a tide table for the Chesapeake Bay and home treatments for illnesses. They learned the names of Supreme Court judges.

After the almanac was printed, Benjamin's life changed. Travelers stopped by his house. They wanted to speak to him and see his clock and worktable. Benjamin welcomed them into his home.

This is the title page of Benjamin's 1792 ALMANACK. There were fewer spelling rules in the 1700s. For example, the word ALMANAC was sometimes spelled with a K on the end.

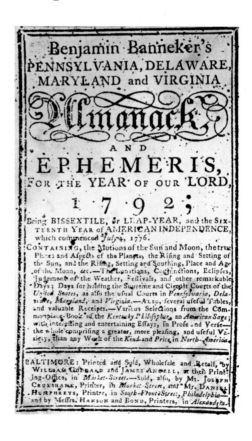

Benjamin published six almanacs from 1792 to 1797. In his *1793 Almanack,* he included the letters sent between Thomas Jefferson and himself. The cover of the *1795 Almanac* had a woodcut portrait of Benjamin.

Banneker's almanacs included news about important events from recent years. His *1795 Almanac* told about the yellow fever illness that struck Philadelphia in 1793.

For some almanacs, Benjamin wrote essays about slavery. He wrote that slavery was wrong and should be stopped. His slavery essays put his life in danger.

This portrait of Benjamin appeared on the cover of the 1795 ALMANAC.

5 FEARS AND DREAMS

Many people in the southern United States did not want to end slavery. They needed slaves to work tobacco and cotton fields. Benjamin must have feared some of his slaveholding neighbors. As an old man, he often had nightmares.

April Fourth Month hath 30 Days

This page, from April 1798, is from Benjamin's journal. He recorded the weather and the movements of the sun and the moon.

He wrote about his dreams in his journal. Once he wrote, "I dreamed I saw some thing passing by my door to and fro ."

By this time, Benjamin was in his sixties. He was too old to grow tobacco. But he kept a small garden, a fruit orchard, and beehives. He let the local boys pick fruit from his orchard. But the boys stripped all the fruit off the trees!

With each passing year, Benjamin's health grew worse. He still lived alone and made his own meals. But two of his sisters helped with the laundry and other chores.

Benjamin was saddened to see his land not being farmed. So he rented some of the land to neighbors. But he had trouble collecting the rent. Sometimes, he forgot to collect it. Other times, his neighbors did not pay.

A few times, he demanded that his neighbors pay the rent. Then they threatened him. In his journal, he once wrote that someone stole his horse and coat. Another time, he wrote that someone wanted to murder him. That person warned him not to let anyone in his house after dark. At times, he heard gunshots outside his cabin.

Benjamin lived in the cabin that his parents built at Stout. It may have looked like the cabin in this picture.

By 1799, Benjamin had sold the rest of his land to the Ellicotts. But they still let him live in his cabin. At night, he wrapped himself in his cloak. He kept looking at the stars. He thought about other planets where people might be living.

BANNEKER'S PUZZLES

All during his life, Benjamin collected puzzles. Many were math puzzles. People often went to the Ellicott & Company store with puzzles for him. The "Puzzle about Cattle" was found in his journal. It tells of a servant getting money (100 pounds) to buy 100 animals. The servant was to spend 5 pounds for each bull, 20 shillings for each cow, and 1 shilling for each sheep. If 20 shillings equals 1 pound, how many of each animal did he buy? (Answer on page 48.)

Benjamin always found something to keep him busy. He watched the bees working in the hive and collected math puzzles. He wrote often in his journal.

Each morning, he took a walk to see the hills he loved. On the morning of October 9, 1806, he took his last walk. After meeting a friend, he began to feel ill. He went home to his couch and died. He was seventy-four years old.

Benjamin Banneker spent a lifetime being curious about the world around him. He did not think of himself as a great man. But he was. He used his talents and kept learning until the day he died.

Timeline

In the year . . .

1737 Benjamin's father, Robert, purchased a farm called Stout. Age 6

1753 Benjamin made a wooden clock.

1759 his father died. Age 28
Benjamin took over the farm.

1763 he bought his first book, the Bible.

1771 he met the Ellicotts and supplied their workers with food. Age 40

1788 he began studying astronomy with George Ellicott's books and instruments. Age 57

1789 he sent George Ellicott his work on the solar eclipse.

1790 he created his first ephemeris but failed to get it published.

1791 he helped Andrew Ellicott with the survey of Washington, D.C. Age 60
he wrote a letter to Thomas Jefferson.
his first almanac was published.

1797 his last almanac was published. Age 66

1799 he sold his farm to the Ellicotts.

1806 he died at home on October 9. Age 74

DIGGING UP BANNEKER'S HOMESITE

Soon after Benjamin died, his family returned George Ellicott's books, instruments, and table from Benjamin's cabin. On the day Benjamin was buried, the cabin burned to the ground in a fire. Most of his belongings were destroyed.

For years, only a few people remembered Benjamin Banneker. But on February 15, 1980, the U.S. Postal Service issued a postage stamp in his honor. In 1985, the Benjamin Banneker Historical Park was created on the site of Benjamin's home. Since then, archaeologists have been digging up objects from the site to learn more about him. Because of these efforts, Benjamin Banneker will always be remembered.

This 1980 postage stamp honored Benjamin's work as a surveyor.

Benjamin Banneker

Black Heritage USA 15c

FURTHER READING

Johnston, Joyce. *Washington, D.C.* **Minneapolis: Lerner Publications Company, 2002.** In this book, you will learn more about the nation's capital.

Lee, Fran. *Wishing on a Star's Constellation, Stories and Stargazing Activities.* **Layton, UT: Gibbs Smith, 2001.** This is a fun book of activities, science facts, and stories from around the world.

Love, Ann, and Jane Drake. *The Kids Book of the Night Sky.* **Toronto: Kids Can Press, 2004.** Learn about the night sky through activities, science, history, legends, and jokes.

Sherrow, Victoria. *Thomas Jefferson.* **Minneapolis: Lerner Publications Company, 2002.** Find out more about Thomas Jefferson in this book.

Stillman, Janice. *The Old Farmer's Almanac for Kids.* **Dublin, NH: Yankee Publishing, 2005.** This book has fun stories, facts, and activities about the heavens.

WEBSITES

Africans in America: Historical Document: "Banneker's Letter to Jefferson 1791."
http://www.pbs.org/wgbh/aia/part2/2h71.html This page has a summary of Benjamin's 1791 letter to Thomas Jefferson and a link to the text of the actual letter.

Africans in America: Historical Document. "Jefferson's Reply to Banneker 1791."
http://www.pbs.org/wgbh/aia/part2/2h72.html This Web page features a summary of Jefferson's reply to Benjamin's 1791 letter and a link to the text of Jefferson's letter.

American Memory (Library of Congress) African American Odyssey *Benjamin Banneker's Pennsylvania, Delaware, Maryland and Virginia Almanack and Ephemeris, for the YEAR of Our Lord 1792*
http://memory.loc.gov/rbc/rbcmisc/ody/ody0214/0214001r.jpg
View the title page of Benjamin's 1792 almanac at this site.

Predicting Weather in the Eighteenth Century
http://www.history.org/History/teaching/weather.cfm This lesson explores how almanacs and weather vanes were used in colonial times.

SELECT BIBLIOGRAPHY

Banneker, Benjamin. *Banneker's Almanack, and Ephemeris, for the Year of Our Lord 1793* and *Banneker's Almanack for the Year of Our Lord 1795.* Afro-American History series. Maxwell Whiteman, ed. Philadelphia: Rhistoric Publications, No. 202.

Bedini, Silvio A. *The Life of Benjamin Banneker: The First African-American Man of Science.* 2nd ed. Baltimore: Maryland Historical Society, 1999.

Bowling, Kenneth R. T*he Creation of Washington, D.C.: The Idea and Location of the American Capital.* Fairfax, VA: George Mason University Press, 1991.

Cerami, Charles. *Benjamin Banneker: Surveyor, Astronomer, Publisher, Patriot.* New York: John Wiley & Sons, 2002.

Ducas, George, ed. *Great Documents in Black American History.* New York: Praeger Publishers, 1970.

INDEX

Answer to Bannker's puzzle: 19 bulls, 1 cow, and 80 sheep.

Acknowledgments

For photographs and artwork: © MPI/Hulton Archive/Getty Images, p. 4; Courtesy
of the Maryland State Archives, Baltimore County Court (Land Records), p. 7;
© The Bridgeman Art Library/Getty Images, p. 9; Schomburg Center for Research in
Black Culture, The New York Public Library, Astor, Lenox and Tilden Foundations,
pp. 10, 19, 41; © EDIFICE/Alamy, p. 11; Division of Work and Industry, National
Museum of American History, Smithsonian Institution, p. 12; Library of Congress,
pp. 16 (LC-USZ62-136120), 17, 26 (LC-USZ62-98345), 31 (LC-USZ62-58124), 35
(LC-MSS-2774821), 36 (LC-USZ62-54696); The Maryland Historical Society,
Baltimore, pp. 18, 24, 33, 38; © Sir James Thornhill/The Bridgeman Art
Library/Getty Images, p. 22; © Bettmann/CORBIS, p. 23; The Historical Society of
Pennsylvania (HSP), p. 27; © North Wind Picture Archives, p. 28; Physical Sciences
Collection, National Museum of American History, Smithsonian Institution, pp. 29,
30; The Granger Collection, New York, pp. 37, 40, 45.

Front Cover: Courtesy of the Banneker-Douglass Museum, Annapolis, Maryland.
Back Cover: © Bettmann/CORBIS.

For quoted material: p.14, Sylvio A. Bedini. The Life of Benjamin Banneker: The
First African-American Man of Science. 2nd ed. Baltimore: Maryland Historical
Society (1999), p. 161; p. 16, Bedini, p. 348.